THE BEST
DOGS
EVER

ROTTWEILERS ARE THE BEST!

Elaine Landau

LERNER PUBLICATIONS COMPANY · MINNEAPOLIS

For Barbara Stripling

Lerner Publications Company
A division of Lerner Publishing Group, Inc.
241 First Avenue North
Minneapolis, MN 55401 U.S.A.

Website address: www.lernerbooks.com

Library of Congress Cataloging-in-Publication Data

Landau, Elaine.
    Rottweilers are the best!/by Elaine Landau.
    p.   cm. — (The best dogs ever)
    Includes index.
    ISBN 978-0-7613-5059-0 (lib. bdg.: alk. paper)
    1. Rottweiler dog—Juvenile literature. I. Title.
  SF429.R7L36 2011
  636.73—dc22   2009037559

Manufactured in the United States of America
1 — BP — 7/15/10

TABLE OF CONTENTS

CHAPTER ONE

THAT SPECIAL DOG

Would having a large, powerful dog appeal to you? The huge pooch I'm thinking of is brave and bold. This dog is also loyal and a true friend. It's a **Rottweiler**. People call these dogs Rotties for short.

A Great Big Beautiful Dog

Rotties are handsome woofers. They stand from 22 to 27 inches (56 to 69 centimeters) tall at the shoulder. Males weigh about 110 pounds (50 kilograms). Females are a little smaller. They weigh about 92 pounds (42 kg).

A Rotty's colors might make you think of Halloween. These dogs are mostly black with rusty orange markings on their face, chest, and legs.

Rottweilers are strong, sleek dogs.

A Pooch to Smooch?

You may have heard scary stories about Rotties. That's because some poorly bred and trained Rotties have had behavior problems. But this is not true for most of these dogs. They are not bred to fight.

LET ME GET TO KNOW YOU

Visiting a friend who has a Rotty? Don't expect this dog to greet you at the door with a big wet kiss. Rotties may not be overly friendly at first. These canines need time to warm up to a person. But few dogs are more devoted to their owners.

A well-bred Rotty is good natured and even tempered. It is also smart, hardworking, and sure of itself. Though large, these dogs are still gentle and playful. They love being petted and cuddled by their owners. Their owners think Rotties are the best dogs ever!

WHAT WOULD BE A GOOD NAME?

People give Rottweilers all kinds of names. See if any of these names fit your Rotty.

SPIKE

Rusty   Buster

TARZAN   Caesar

DOLLY   CAPTAIN

Muffin   Kisses

CHAPTER TWO
WHAT A HISTORY!

Rottweilers have a long history. The Roman army used dogs like them. They traveled with the troops across Europe. These dogs herded the cattle the army used for meat. They also guarded the soldiers' camps at night.

This Roman mosaic shows a guard dog. Do you think it could be a Rotty?

At the time, many butchers used these dogs too. Rotties pulled the butchers' meat carts to market. Some people say the butchers put their money in a small purse tied around the dog's neck. This kept the money safe from robbers along the way.

This mosaic shows Roman men hunting with sturdy, bold dogs.

In this picture from the early 1900s, a dog helps its owner to deliver milk.

Modern Times

Modern-day Rotties got their start in Germany. They were brought to the United States in the late 1920s. The U.S. Army used them in wartime. They also made fine police dogs. Rotties were trained as search and rescue dogs as well.

Rotties get their name from the town of Rottweil in Germany.

LIFESAVERS

During World War I (1914–1918), some Rotties showed great bravery. They went out on the battlefield to find wounded soldiers. The Rotties ignored all the action going on around them. They helped save lives.

The Rottweiler above (*bottom corner, lying down*) helped Red Cross workers find a wounded soldier during World War I.

Yet Rotties are more than working dogs. They proved to be good pets too. They became especially popular in the 1980s. Well-trained Rotties are a good fit with many families.

A Working Dog

The American Kennel Club (AKC) groups different types of dogs by breed. Breeds that have some things in common are grouped together. Some AKC groups are the toy group, the hound group, and the sporting group.

This Afghan hound is in the hound group.

The English springer spaniel is part of the sporting group.

The Yorkshire terrier is part of the toy group.

This Rottweiler helps its owner at home.

Some Rotties are trained as therapy dogs. These dogs are taken to hospitals and nursing homes. They cheer up the patients there.

Akitas are in the working group, just like Rotties.

Rotties are in the working group. All the dogs in this group are large, smart, and strong. Other working-group dogs are the boxer and the Akita.

CHAPTER THREE

THE RIGHT DOG FOR YOU?

Like the idea of strutting down the street with a great-looking dog? Think a Rotty might be the right dog for you? Well, don't rush out to get one. These dogs are not for everyone. Read on to see if a Rotty is right for you.

Is There Space at Your Place?

A Rotty is not a little pooch. It needs room to stretch out and relax. These dogs also need space to run and play. A Rotty would not do well in a small apartment.

No Couch Potatoes, Please

Rotties are active dogs. They need lots of exercise. Do you like to run, hike, and swim? Your Rotty can do all these things with you. Rotties should also be walked for thirty minutes at least twice a day.

Home Alone? A Rotten Idea for Rotties

Rotties need company. They want to be with their human family. These dogs should not be left alone all day. A lonely, bored Rotty is an unhappy pet. It may chew on household items and bark until someone comes home.

A bored Rotty can make a big mess while you're out!

Time for Training

Rotties are powerful dogs. They are also very strong willed. They must be well trained to make good family pets. Nothing is more important with this breed. Training should begin while your dog is still a puppy. Low-cost training classes exist in many areas. If you don't have time to train a Rotty, don't get one.

TRAIN YOUR PET WELL

All dogs must learn basic commands. This is especially important for large dogs. Basic commands include sit, stay, down, come, and stand. Large dogs must also learn not to jump up on people. A 110-pound (50 kg) dog can easily knock over a small child. These dogs must learn to walk on a leash without pulling as well. You should walk your dog—your dog should not walk you!

Find the Perfect Pooch

Getting a well-bred Rotty is very important. This means getting your dog from a known and trusted source. Even-tempered, stable Rotties make super pets.

Responsible Rottweiler breeders are a good source for finding a Rotty.

LOYAL AND LOVING

Rotties often get very close to their special humans and want to protect them. Yet these playful pooches also like to clown around. Some people say that Rotties have a great sense of humor.

Is a Rotty right for you? If so, get set for loads of love and tons of fun. A great pooch is coming your way.

Rotties are fun-loving dogs!

CHAPTER FOUR

HOME SWEET HOME

The big day is finally here. You're getting the dog of your dreams. Your Rotty is coming home to stay.

It's fine to be happy and excited. But it's really important to be ready. Get the basic items you'll need before you get your dog. The list below will help you get started.

- collar

- leash

- tags (for identification)

- dog food

- food and water bowls

- crates (one for when your pet travels by car and one for it to rest in at home)

- treats (to be used in training)

- toys

Get to a Vet

Take your dog to a veterinarian right away. That's a doctor who treats animals. People call them vets for short.

The vet will check your dog's health and give it the shots it needs. Take your dog back to the vet for checkups. Also take your dog to the vet if it gets sick.

This vet is pointing out a break in a dog's leg bone. Vets help you keep your dog healthy.

Regular exercise will help your Rotty stay happy and healthy.

Don't feed your Rotty table scraps. This can lead to weight gain and health problems. Use dog treats for training, not as snacks.

Good Grooming

Rotties have double coats. This means they have two layers of fur. One layer is soft and woolly. It lies close to the dog's skin. The other layer is straight and coarse. It grows over the softer layer.

A Rotty's coat shines in the sun.

Brush your dog once a week to remove dead hair. Bathe your Rotty about every other month. Also clip its nails when they get too long.

Be careful when clipping your Rotty's nails. Cutting them too short can hurt a dog.

Regular brushing and bathing will keep your Rotty's coat healthy.

You and Your Rotty

Be good to your Rotty. Make it feel like a member of the family. Many Rotties follow their owners around the house. Don't be surprised if your dog sits at your side when you do your homework or watch TV.

YOURS FOR YEARS

With proper care, most Rotties live for nine to twelve years. Some have lived even longer.

Don't forget about your dog when you're busy. Your Rotty still needs you. Give it the hugs and love it needs. Your Rotty will be your best friend. Be its best friend as well.

GLOSSARY

American Kennel Club (AKC): an organization that groups dogs by breed. The AKC also defines the characteristics of different breeds.

breed: a particular type of dog. Dogs of the same breed have the same body shape and general features. *Breed* can also refer to producing puppies.

canine: a dog, or having to do with dogs

coat: a dog's fur

herd: to make animals move together as a group

search and rescue dog: a dog that finds people after disasters

therapy dog: a dog brought to nursing homes or hospitals to comfort patients

veterinarian: a doctor who treats animals. Veterinarians are called vets for short.

working group: a group of dogs that were bred to do different types of jobs, such as guarding property, carrying messages, or pulling sleds

FOR MORE INFORMATION

Books

Bozzo, Linda. *My First Dog*. Berkeley Heights, NJ: Enslow Publishers, 2008. This book offers readers some basic advice on dogs, including the best places to find a dog.

Brecke, Nicole, and Patricia M. Stockland. *Dogs You Can Draw*. Minneapolis: Millbrook Press, 2010. Perfect for dog lovers, this colorful book teaches readers how to draw many different popular dog breeds.

Fiedler, Julie. *Rottweilers*. New York: PowerKids Press, 2006. This book tells about the Rottweiler's history as well as its important role as a working dog.

Gray, Susan H. *Rottweilers*. Mankato, MN: Child's World, 2008. Readers will find a close-up look at Rottweilers in this book.

Landau, Elaine. *Your Pet Dog*. Rev. ed. New York: Children's Press, 2007. This title is a good guide for young people on choosing and caring for a dog.

Websites

American Kennel Club
http://www.akc.org
Visit this website to find a complete listing of AKC-registered dog breeds, including the Rottweiler. This site also features fun printable activities for kids.

ASPCA Animaland
http://www2.aspca.org/site/PageServer?pagename=kids_pc_home
Check out this page for helpful hints on caring for a dog and other pets.

FBI Working Dogs
http://www.fbi.gov/kids/dogs/doghome.htm
This fun site tells how dogs in the working group help the Federal Bureau of Investigation (FBI).

Index

Photo Acknowledgments

The images in this book are used with the permission of: backgrounds © iStockphoto.com/Julie Fisher and © iStockphoto.com/Tomasz Adamczyk; © iStockphoto.com/Michael Balderas, p. 1; © Eric Isselée/Dreamstime.com, pp. 4, 12 (main and right inset); © Cynoclub/Dreamstime.com, pp. 5, 16, 18–19, 19, 26 (top); © Ronnie Kaufman/CORBIS, p. 6 (top); © Mike Pease/St. Petersburg Times/ZUMA Press, p. 6 (bottom); © Hou Guima/Dreamstime.com, p. 7; Erich Lessing/Art Resource, NY, pp. 8, 9 (top); © Jupiterimages/Thinkstock/Getty Images, p. 9 (bottom); © imagebroker/Alamy, pp. 10 (top), 29; © Paul Thompson/FPG/Hulton Archive/Getty Images, p. 10 (bottom); © Robert Llewellyn/ Workbook Stock/Getty Images, p. 11; © Erik Lam/Shutterstock Images, p. 12 (left inset); SOUTH COAST PRESS/Rex Features USA, p. 13 (top); © Dave King/Dorling Kindersley/Getty Images, p. 13 (bottom); © Sunheyy/Dreamstime.com, p. 14; © Emiliano Rodriguez/Alamy, p. 15; © Arsty/Dreamstime.com, p. 17 (top); © Corbis/Photolibrary, p. 17 (bottom); © iStockphoto.com/Catherine Lane, p. 18; © Sherry Piatti/ Dreamstime.com, p. 20; © Stana-Fotolia.com, p. 21 (top); © GK Hart/Vikki Hart/Brad X Pictures/Getty Images, p. 21 (bottom); © iStockphoto.com/surely, pp. 22, 23 (bottom); © Tammy Mcallister/Dreamstime .com, p. 23 (top); © April Turner/Dreamstime.com, p. 23 (2nd from top); © iStockphoto.com/orix3, p. 23 (2nd from bottom); © Larry Reynolds/dogpix.com, p. 24 (top); © Juniors Bildarchiv/Photolibrary, p. 24 (bottom); © Flirt/SuperStock, p. 25; © Davekinder/Dreamstime.com, p. 26 (bottom); © Tatiana Makotra/Dreamstime.com, p. 27 (top); © Michael Brown/Dreamstime.com, p. 27 (bottom); © Jerry Shulman/SuperStock, p. 28 (top); © iStockphoto.com/Nikolay Titov, p. 28 (bottom).

Front cover: © Cynoclub/Dreamstime.com.
Back cover: © Eric Isselée/Dreamstime.com.